First World War
and Army of Occupation
War Diary
France, Belgium and Germany

62 DIVISION
186 Infantry Brigade
Hampshire Regiment
2/4th (T.F.) Battalion
1 June 1918 - 28 February 1919

WO95/3087/3

The Naval & Military Press Ltd
www.nmarchive.com
Published in association with The National Archives

Published by

The Naval & Military Press Ltd

Unit 10 Ridgewood Industrial Park,

Uckfield, East Sussex,

TN22 5QE England

Tel: +44 (0) 1825 749494

www.naval-military-press.com

www.nmarchive.com

This diary has been reprinted in facsimile from the original. Any imperfections are inevitably reproduced and the quality may fall short of modern type and cartographic standards.

© **Crown Copyright**
Images reproduced by permission of The National Archives, London, England, 2015.

Contents

Document type	Place/Title	Date From	Date To
Heading	WO95/3087-3		
Heading	62nd Division 186th Infy Bde 2-4th Bn Hampshire Regt. 1918 Jun-1919 Feb From Egypt 75 Div 233 Bde To 29 Div 88 Bde		
Heading	War Diary of 2/4th Hampshire Regt. From 1st June 1918 To 30 June 1918 Volume 12		
War Diary	B.E.F.	01/06/1918	22/06/1918
Heading	186th Brigade 62nd Division 2/4th Bn. Hampshire Regt. July 1918		
Heading	War Diary of 2/4th Hampshire Regiment Period 1st July To 31st July 1918 Volume No.13		
War Diary	B.E.F.	01/07/1918	31/07/1918
Heading	War Diary of 2/4 Hampshire Regt. From Aug 1st 1918 To Aug 31st 1918 Vol. No. 14		
War Diary	In The Field	01/08/1918	31/08/1918
Operation(al) Order(s)	Operation Order No.1	26/08/1918	26/08/1918
Heading	War Diary 2/4th Battn Hampshire Regt. From September 1st 1918 To September 30th 1918 Vol 4		
War Diary		01/09/1918	30/09/1918
Miscellaneous	Operation Order By Lieut Col F. Broch Dome Comdg 2/4 Hants Regt	11/09/1918	11/09/1918
Heading	War Diary 2/4 Hampshire Regiment From 1-10-18 To 31-10-18 Vol. XVII		
War Diary		01/10/1918	31/10/1918
Miscellaneous	2-4th Hampshire Regiment Narrative of Operations from 19th October 1918 to 22nd October 1918	26/10/1918	26/10/1918
Operation(al) Order(s)	2/4 Hampshire Regiment Operation Order No. II	18/10/1918	18/10/1918
Miscellaneous	Copy of Letter from Lt. Col. Brook Re 2/4th Hants	13/10/1918	13/10/1918
Miscellaneous	2/4th Battn. Hampshire Regiment Narrative of Operations from 27th Septr to 1st October 1918	01/10/1918	01/10/1918
Heading	War Diary of 2/4 Hampshire Regiment From 1.11.18 To 30.11.18 Vol 6		
War Diary		25/11/1918	30/11/1918
Miscellaneous	2/4th Battalion Hampshire Regiment Narrative of Operations 3rd to 11th November 1918	11/11/1918	11/11/1918
Heading	War Diary of 2/4 Hampshire Regiment Volume 18 From December 1st 1918 To December 31st 1918 Vol 7		
War Diary	Barcenal (Belgium)	01/12/1918	17/12/1918
War Diary	(Germany)	22/12/1918	31/12/1918
Heading	War Diary of 2/4th Battalion The Hampshire Regiment From January 1st 1919 To January 31st 1919 Vol 8		
War Diary	Mechernich (Germany)	00/01/1919	00/01/1919
Heading	War Diary of 2/4th Battalion The Hampshire Regiment Period From 1-2-1919 To 28-2-1919 Volume No.21		
War Diary	Mechernich	01/02/1919	23/02/1919
War Diary	Wermelskirchen	24/02/1919	28/02/1919
Miscellaneous	D.A.V.S 1919		

No 95/3087(3)

MS4/3087(3)

62ND DIVISION
186TH INFY BDE

2-4TH BN HAMPSHIRE REGT
~~JUN - DEC 1918~~
1918 JUN — 1919 FEB

FROM EGYPT
75 DIV 233 BDE

To 29 DIV 88 BDE

SECRET.

ORIGINAL. 186/62

WAR DIARY

of

2/4TH HAMPSHIRE REGT.

VOLUME 12.

From :— 1st June 1918.
To :— 30 June 1918.

T.12

J.D.L.Shuhah Lieut Colonel
Commanding 2/4th Hampshire Regiment

ORIGINAL
2/4 Hunt Regt

Army Form C. 2118.

WAR DIARY
or
INTELLIGENCE SUMMARY.
(Erase heading not required.)

Place	Date	Hour	Summary of Events and Information	Remarks and references to Appendices
B.E.F.	1.		Battalion arrived MARSEILLES and went into Camp - No 10 Rest Camp.	App
	2		Entrained at MARSEILLES for DOULLENS.	App
	5		Arrived DOULLENS, march to AMPLIER, thei Battalion went into camp	App
	6		Major Gen W.P. Braithwaite C.B. Commanding 62 (West Riding) Divn. inspected Battalion	App
	8		Major R.S.J. Parsons 15 Offrs 97 O.Rs proceeded to trenches for instruction - attached 187 Bde	App
			Lt Col. H.B.L. Stencell 9 Offrs 62 O.Rs proceeded to trenches for instruction - attached 186 Bde	
	10		K.H.C.B. Cottam assumed command of 'B' Coy. vice Captain A.C. Ashman	App
	14		Captain maskery R.A.M.C. posted for duty	
	15		Battalion proceeded to BOUZINCOURT by motor bus and relieved 2/7th Duke of Wellington Regt in support line in right Brigade sector	App
	16		Lt. Col. W.H.L. Wilder & 2.C. hours proceeded ORVILLE for leave. Enemy bombarded B.H.Q. & Bn scheme of defence being altered. Bn moved into new alloted positions B.H.Q. being in PIGEON WOOD E.30.A.2.6.	App
			Cotton C.P. Battery proceeded to MARCONELLE for Gas Course.	App

Army Form C. 2118.

WAR DIARY
or
INTELLIGENCE SUMMARY.

Original
1/4 Hants Regt

(Erase heading not required.)

Place	Date	Hour	Summary of Events and Information	Remarks and references to Appendices
B.E.F.	16		Captain W.S. Came & 73 O.Rs proceeded to ORVILLE to ... Gun School	
	17		C and E Companies proceeded to relieve 2 Coys of 7th N Bucks of Wellington Regt and the rest of	
	18		H.Q. and B & N Companies relieved H.Q. and remaining Coys of the 1/5 Bush of Wellington	
	20		Lt.-Col. C.M. Cumming RAMC relieved Captain MacKenzie	
	23		Capt. H.W. FitzGerald proceeded on leave to England	
	24		Lieut. L.R.D. Conant proceeded on leave to England	
			Captain C.A. Bailey returned from MARTONETTE from Gas Course	
			Battalion relieved by the 10th Royal Fusiliers and marched to Camp at HENU	
	26		Lt. M.E. Willette & 90 spares reported from ORVILLE	
			Draft 96 O.Rs arrived from Base	
			Captain P.S. Skurai to Hospital	
	27		Captain Curran Cater proceeding on leave to England	
	28		Lieut. A. Scott	
			Captain CP Butler proceeded on leave to England	
	29		Lt. R.M. Grotrian & Lt. H.R. Bryant proceeded to PORT MAHON to 3rd Army School	
			Casualties	
	17		1 O.R. (wounded)	
	18		1	
	19		2	
	20		1	
	27			

Commanding 1/4th Hampshire Regt

186th Brigade,

62nd Division.

2/4th Bn. HAMPSHIRE REGT.

J U L Y, 1 9 1 8.

SECRET. ORIGINAL.

T.13

WAR DIARY.

OF

2/4TH HAMPSHIRE REGIMENT.

PERIOD:- 1ST JULY TO 31ST JULY 1918.

VOLUME No.13.

F.Krogh
Lieut-Colonel
Commanding 2/4th Hampshire Regiment.

WAR DIARY
or
INTELLIGENCE SUMMARY.

Army Form C. 2118.

2/4 HAMPSHIRE Regt

Place	Date	Hour	Summary of Events and Information	Remarks and references to Appendices
B.E.F.	1.		Battalion in camp at HENU. Carrying out a course of Training, musketry &c.	B/P
	2.		2nd Lieut H. WILLIHER and 3 O.R. proceeded to L.G. School ORVILLE. 2nd Lieut P.S. SKUSE returned to duty from hospital. Capt. R.L. STILWELL proceeded on 30 days leave to ENGLAND and Major	B/P
	3.		B.E.T. PARSONS assumed Command of the Battalion	B/P
			The Battalion found the Divisional guard at PAS. 6th relieved in the 75 mit?	B/P
	4.		2/Lieut E.H. WORKMAN proceeded on leave to ENGLAND	B/P
	6.		8 O.R. proceeded to Divisional School ORVILLE for junior N.C.O.s Course.	B/P
	7.		Lt A. SCOTT returned from le HAVRE.	B/P
	8.		Demonstration of P Company in the attack under direction of the R.O.C. Lt Bn/Maj B/P	
			Capt N.H. LEDGARD returned from leave and Capt W.S. CAVE proceeded on leave to ENGLAND.	B/P

Army Form C. 2118.

Original
1st Hampshire Regt

WAR DIARY
or
INTELLIGENCE SUMMARY.
(Erase heading not required)

Instructions regarding War Diaries and Intelligence Summaries are contained in F. S. Regs., Part II. and the Staff Manual respectively. Title pages will be prepared in manuscript.

Place	Date	Hour	Summary of Events and Information	Remarks and references to Appendices
B.E.F.	9		LIEUT H. BROWN and 2/Lieut H.L. THURGOOD reported to the Battalion for duty.	App
	10		2/Lt F.C. ISAACS proceeded on leave to ENGLAND and Lt L.R.T. COWARD returned. 2/Lt Viscount UFFINGTON rejoined for duty from hospital.	App App
	11		2/Lt A.S. WEEKS proceeded on leave to ENGLAND.	App
	12		Capt. P.S. SKUSE proceeded on leave to ENGLAND	App
	14		Major J. BROOK D.S.O. M.C. Yorkshire L.I. assumed command of Battalion.	App
	15.		Advance party A.B.& D coys entrained at MONDICOURT at 3 a.m. destination unknown. C. coy as surrounded working party and followed by late train - arrived SONNESOUS at 12 pm & proceeded in motor lorries to AUTHIS where Battalion was billeted.	App App
	16.			App

A5834. Wt. W.4973/M687 750,000 8/16 D. D. & L. Ltd. "Forms/C.2118/13.

WAR DIARY or INTELLIGENCE SUMMARY

Army Form C. 2118.

1/4th Hampshire Regt

Place	Date	Hour	Summary of Events and Information	Remarks and references to Appendices
B.E.F.	17		Battalion remained AUTHIS. MAJOR G.J.M. MOLYNEUX D.S.O. Hampshire Regt. Assumed command of duty. CAPT. C.P. BULLEY returned from leave.	
	18.		Battalion continued at AUTHIS	
	19.	5:30 am	Battalion marched to GERMAINE. Commanding Officer & Company Commanders proceeded on Reconnaissance	
	19.	11pm	Battalion left for area by Motor Lorry to attack near CURTAGNON FARM.	
	20. Jan		The Brown commenced its attack — 86 Brigade having as its objective CONTAGNON to Bottom cross road. Very early this Bn had to deploy — 3 Battalions this morning support to its Brigade — 3 Battalions in line this Battalion being on its left. Battalion immediately on reaching CONTAGNON to Bottom cross road. MAJOR MOLYNEUX Distinguished himself this Stage & dressed forward. Enemy artillery increased but the Battn advanced slowly.	

Army Form C. 2118.

WAR DIARY
or
INTELLIGENCE SUMMARY.
(Erase heading not required.)

Original
7th Hunts[hire?] Regt

Place	Date	Hour	Summary of Events and Information	Remarks and references to Appendices
			At POZIÈRES being attached, it was found that the 1st Bn had had little progress toward MARTINPUICH and KEBURY was still under enemy M.G. fire. The attack was continued B Coy heading with A Coy in support, it was found impossible to reach MARTINPUICH due to enfilade M.G. fire in spite of the bravery of all ranks it was impossible to reach MARTINPUICH due to enemy machine guns. It was found that the village of the high ground overlooking the valley with numerous M.G. in all turns managed to rake positions but the front was maintained as a the OUTSKIRTS about 500 yds to E of the village. The ammunition was carried out successfully by stout hearted [?] B.H.Q. was ordered to keep Artillery M.G. & also day - at nightfall the companies were withdrawn. A B Coy holding front line & F Coys were in support. Batt HQ at POZIÈRES. Casualties being - Killed 2/Lt N.E. SMITH & Wounded MAJOR S.P. MOLYNEUX - LIEUT A. SCOTT 2/Lt SNODDY 2/Lt MULLISH 2/Lt E.L. THURTFORD 2/Lt H.C. BUD[?] SICK 2/Lt T.F.T DRAKE	

A 5831. Wt. W4973/M687 730,000 8/16 D. D. & L. Ltd. Forms/C.2118/13.

WAR DIARY
INTELLIGENCE SUMMARY

Army Form C. 2118.

Place	Date	Hour	Summary of Events and Information	Remarks and references to Appendices
B.E.F.	21.		Situation unchanged. Batt. remained holding its position - being heavily shelled most of the day - "C" Coy. arrived B.S. H.Q. from MAILLY. Front the Batt. at 9 pm -	
	22.		Batt. continued to hold its position - Attack on the hill Bois de Petits Champs being carried out by another Batt. Heavy shell fire continued. During the night orders received for B Coy to attack MARFAUX in conjunction with N.Z. Cyclist Corps. Formed up place astride BIGGY - MARFAUX Road.	
	23.		ZERO hour was 8 am. a very good barrage was put down. full advance pushed forward 9 the village was soon in our hands. 8 M.G. & 30 prisoners were taken. Drove on consolidated 500 yards N.W of the village. Capt. W.A. LEDGARD received a bad shrapnel wound & a very gallant officer called on	
			CASUALTIES. KILLED. O.R. DIED OF WOUNDS Lieut C.F. MASON. Capt. W. A. LEDGARD ? O.R.	

WAR DIARY or INTELLIGENCE SUMMARY

Army Form C. 2118.

Place	Date	Hour	Summary of Events and Information	Remarks and references to Appendices
BEF	24		Situation unchanged. The Battalion was again subjected to heavy shell fire for a considerable period & gas shells & incendiary.	
	25		During night C Coy was withdrawn from front line & N.7 MAR-FAUX App into BOIS de POURCY. The N.Z. Cyclists being left in their place. 2/Lt C.A. GADSBY & 25 O.R's of 1/4 th Bn. R. Berks. W'D. as reinforcements for Bn.	App
	26		Battalion relieved N.Z. Cyclists in ST. MARTFAUX, C Coy holding & advancing posts with A, B & D Coys (one coy) in support	App
	27		In conjunction with an attack on the S towards BUIRE HQRE 5/1 N.Z. Division. The Batt was ordered to push forward a British a line N C.44.b.11.12.7.3 thru the village & was seen to be in British hands. C" Coy was ordered to carry out the operation. At early morning Coy's Bombers carried out a daylight patrol & a result of which the enemy was seen retiring from BOIS, and the Coy then proceeded to make good in support Batt H.Q. also pushed forward & at MAR-FAUX.	App

WAR DIARY or INTELLIGENCE SUMMARY

Army Form C. 2118.

Place	Date	Hour	Summary of Events and Information	Remarks and references to Appendices
B.E.F.	27		during the afternoon the CORPS CAVALRY came through and at 7.30 pm the Batt^n were again ordered to move forward following up the Cavalry. By this time night saw was falling & the men tired out.	O.C. was M Humphries
	28		further came in during Coulevalin with Cavalry on either flank, & by midnight the Battn had reached STN STABOUL, 4/5/P 6 kilometres E.I. BLICNY. Cavalry line at 9 pm immediately E.I. BLICNY 740 At 2.20 am orders were received that the Battn should go again attack BLIGNY & our Brigade was to be the Objective. Battn HQ had moved forward to CHOURUZY. ZERO hr 4.30 am but it was impossible to get ahead prepared by that time & the start was late. Battn officers were all completely done for by this, had a magnificent effort to get forward. A, B & D coys went to late BLIGNY. C coy to come round and establish here & pass on final objective. The line of advance was swept by adrenant fire from rt & bt, machine guns from F. Battn & by heavy Artillery ... advance.

WAR DIARY
or
INTELLIGENCE SUMMARY
(Erase heading not required.)

Army Form C. 2118.

Original
5th Hunfordshire Regt

Place	Date	Hour	Summary of Events and Information	Remarks and references to Appendices
BEF	28		Owing to moving 2/Lt HOLBROOK & 2 O.R. wounded in getting forward & Lewis village before direct opposition. Our party established itself in N.E. end of village & have stay lying on all day. The Battn on our Right had failed to move any forward and our Right flank was in the air, but two effort to get round about continued.	
		4 p.m.	Fresh attempt was made by Bomb: Division & Lewis gun along ability of ARDAL onwards. Westerly of 1st BRIGR & 2/Lt VICKERSON & 2 ordr WILLIAMS carrying on to KRPS reconnaissance. At 4 p.m. were to attached also to three DSO & also & for the return home to by 5 p.m. fine that from PALEL, BLIGNY were & the new line consolidated. On this being reported to 186 Brigade following message was received from G.O.C. "Tell your Officers & men they have done splendidly. During night 28/29 the Battn was relieved by 1st K.O.Y.L.I. and withdrew who support of CHAUMUZY.	

Army Form C. 2118.

Original
2/4 Hampshire Regt

WAR DIARY
or
INTELLIGENCE SUMMARY.
(Erase heading not required.)

Instructions regarding War Diaries and Intelligence Summaries are contained in F. S. Regs., Part II. and the Staff Manual respectively. Title pages will be prepared in manuscript.

Place	Date	Hour	Summary of Events and Information	Remarks and references to Appendices
REF.	29.		Quiet day was spent - new tracking, having thing themselves in an ex bivouac ant. 2/Lt- F.C. ISAACS + 2/Lt H.S. WEEKS returned from leave.	AP AP
	30		Quiet day was spent.	
	31	4.30 pm	Orders received to withdraw to WAGGON hire on GERMAINE- CORTAGNON road which was reached at 9pm. Battalion moved to bivouac on GERMAINE-ST MOGE road.	AP

TOTAL CASUALTIES

KILLED
Officers O.R.
2 33

WOUNDED
Officers O.R.
9 170

MISSING
O.R.
139.

P. Bush.
Lt. Col.
Comd.g
2/4 Hampshire Regt.

SECRET

Original
M 3 16/6
JM

T.14

WAR DIARY
OF
2/4 HAMPSHIRE REGT.

From Aug 1st 1918
To Aug 31st 1918

Vol. No. 14.

J Brooks. Lt Col
2/4 HANTS. REGT.

Vol II Original

August 1915

Army Form C. 2118.

WAR DIARY
or
INTELLIGENCE SUMMARY.

(Erase heading not required.)

2/4 Hampshires

Instructions regarding War Diaries and Intelligence Summaries are contained in F. S. Regs., Part II. and the Staff Manual respectively. Title pages will be prepared in manuscript.

Place	Date	Hour	Summary of Events and Information	Remarks and references to Appendices
In the Field	1/8/18		March past. Gen Berthelot, G.O.C. 5th French Army at EPERNAY. Bn was congratulated by G.O.C. 15 war having made the best impression out of the 2 Divisions in the march past. Billeted at CHOUILLY.	
	4		Entrained at ORIRY, OIRY	
	5.		Arrived at DOULLENS and marched to ST LEGER arriving here at 9.30 pm	
	7.		Lieut. J.C. Holbrook proceeded on leave to U.K.	
	8		" R.P. Jean " "	
	10.		Capt. P.S. Skues Lewis-Plain, R.R. Workman, J Hart, H. Bryant + 85 ORs rejoined Bn from Base	
	15		Lecture given to Bn by Major Conlan a.o.s. on P.+B.2.	
	17.		G. ORs found as reinforcements. Major B.E.J Parsons & S.A Greenhalgh proceeded on leave to U.K.	
	19/20		Marched from ST LEGER to WARLUZEL by night, harassed to VI Corps. arriving 3am and leaving 8.30 pm 20th	
	21		Marched from WARLUZEL to THIEVRES - arriving at 1.30 am returning to N Corps	
	23		Marched from THIEVRES to SAULTY - left at 7.30 pm & arr SAULTY 10.30 pm	
	24		Marched and Bivouced from SAULTY about 7.30am marched via MONCHY to bivouac near AYETTE for some hours. Thence to training ground for 2 hours, where orders were received to proceed here as ACHET-LE-GRAND and be in support on training ground on G.S.C and G.H.A in support of the 5th Infantry Bde.	
	25		Arrived in position at about 2 am near ACHET LEGRAND with headquarters on the railway received to proceed to trenches where the post was established. Orders received to proceed to C.6.6.55 to attack on trench line in B.2.g and 1.16.0 peration order No.1 attached (see appendix I)	Aff I.
	26		The assembly post was reached at 5 am. The great difficulty owing to rain and darkness and no guides being provided. The attack starting at 6am was most was successfully carried out. 1st objective was gained without difficulty except for enemy barrage which was fairly heavy. Considerable difficulty was experienced in getting the final objective owing to heavy M.G. fire from the road and high ground met with beyond this. The Bn was dug in. This was especially so on the left, but Captain Cave took his Coy with considerable skill, and by 9am all objectives were gained and the Bn now forward	

WAR DIARY
INTELLIGENCE SUMMARY

Army Form C. 2118.

August 1918. (Contd)

2/4th Hampshire Regiment

Place	Date	Hour	Summary of Events and Information	Remarks and references to Appendices
	26.		Casualties:- 2Lt. C.B. Richmond wounded. 25 O.R. wounded, 5 O.R. Killed. 5 O.R. Killed. bah: J? Bennell. Killed. Positions taken up as follows:- C.Coy. H.5.c.3.5 to B.29.d.8.4. A.Coy. B.29.a.5.4 (Exclusive) along hedge to B.29.a.5.4 D.Coy. In support to C.Coy also forming a defensive flank with 3 platoons facing south along hedge running thro' H.11.a. and D. B.Coy. In support- to A.Coy. in B.28.d. Captain J? Bennell was killed just as orders went received to move 'C' Coy forward into trench line running from H.6.c.3.5 to B.29.d.8.4. This position was famous about dusk. 2 platoons of B.Coy being pushed into line between A.Coy's right and C.Coy's left. HQ. finally established in dugout B.28.c.4.5. Total Casualties for day, Killed. 1 Officer, 9 O.Rs. wounded 1 Off. 39 O.R. Missing. 7 O.R.	
	27.		Dispositions - Slightly altered. A.Coy remained the same with 3 Platoons in line and 1 in support B - moved all 4 platoons into new position extended from C - doing the same. Items coming thus are below Casualties:- wounded Adjut- J.G. Holbrook. 9 O.Rs. 5. Missing 1 O.R.	
	28.		Patrols were pushed out in the attempt to establish posts along the BAPAUME - VRAUCOURT Road slightly in advance of my present line. B.Coy lost 2 men killed and 1 wounded, Identifying the horse lines and compelling the enemy to withdraw. This patrol was later withdrawn owing to rifle and M.G. fire from enemy concealed N of the HORSE LINES. B.30.a and from E towards VAUCX. 2 Germans were killed and the whole of section 'C' Coy handled towards H.6.c.5.4. S of horse lines and was freed on by rifle and snipers fire. 1 man killed. Several enemy m.c. located on bank running from H.6.c.2.4 to B.25.5.5 right hand Coy's respectively and several causalties occurred. Between 2pm & 6.30pm heavy Enemy shell fire was often followed on B.Coy and C.Coy the centre and right hand Coy's respectively and several casualties occurred.	(C.R.L.)

Army Form C. 2118.

WAR DIARY
or
INTELLIGENCE SUMMARY.
(Erase heading not required.) 2/4 Hampshire Regiment

Instructions regarding War Diaries and Intelligence
Summaries are contained in F. S. Regs., Part II.
and the Staff Manual respectively. Title pages
will be prepared in manuscript.

August 1918

Place	Date	Hour	Summary of Events and Information	Remarks and references to Appendices
	28.		A good deal of gas was sent over but adequate men who were slightly gassed were able to return to duty. Casualties killed O.Rs. 6 wounded O.Rs. 27 Missing O.Rs. 1.	
	29.		At 2 pm 2/Lt H. Brierly with one Platoon from A Coy was ordered to attack the HORSE LINES & which the 1/5 Devons who were advancing at that time, the found Bosches in the HORSE LINES and asked for reinforcements. After this, the commander of B Coy sent up another Platoon. The enemy was driven out and the HORSE LINES held. 2 Platoons consolidated immediately E. of the road. As this point it was seen that the Devons had not yet come up, so another Platoon was sent to cover the left flank. At 5 p.m. the enemy was seen advancing in two to make an attack from a position 500 yds East of the Coy's posts; his attack was at once broken by Lewis Gun & rifle fire, considerable casualties being inflicted. Artillery fire had been asked for which inflicted further casualties on the enemy but unfortunately one or two short shells killed one or two of our own men. At this stage Lt Bayour with his Platoon was brought up. Casualties killed 4 wounded about 10. 21 Boches were captured in the LMk adm and many killed and wounded. 1 Machine Gun and one Granatenwerfer were captured. Casualties during the day killed 5 O.Rs. Wounded 11 O.Rs. Missing 1 O.R.	

Army Form C. 2118.

WAR DIARY
or
INTELLIGENCE SUMMARY.
(Erase heading not required.)

2/4 Hampshire Regt.   Aug. 1918

Instructions regarding War Diaries and Intelligence Summaries are contained in F. S. Regs., Part II. and the Staff Manual respectively. Title pages will be prepared in manuscript.

Place	Date	Hour	Summary of Events and Information	Remarks and references to Appendices
	30.		The Bn was relieved during the night 29/30. by the 2/4 Bn. of W. Rep. Relief completed at 1 am. H.Q. was established at H.2.c.6.4. and Coys were distributed at BEHAGNIES and SAPIGNIES near the Bn. HQs. At 2 pm B & D Coys were ordered into the old positions on the line at B.29.d and N.5.b. respectively. C & A being in support at H.4.c.4.8. and H.4.a.5.5. respectively. Casualties 1 OR killed and 5 wounded.	
	31.		Bn remained in the same positions - in support to 5th 2/4 R of W. Rep. Casualties nil OR wounded	

J. Forsyth, Lieut Colonel
Commanding 2/4 Hampshire Regiment

1.9.18.

Appendix *F*

Operation Order No. 1.

Ref Map. ERVILLERS. (1a. Local)

1. The Battalion will attack the trench line in B.29. & H.6. on the morning of 26th Aug. 1918.

2. Forming up line will be in Sunken Rd H.4.a.2.0. to B.28.c.2.6.

3. Battn. will attack on a two Coy. Front.
   Right Forward Coy. D.
   Left   "   "   B.
   Right Rear   "   C.
   Left   "   "   A.

4. First Objective will be Gird line between H.5 & H.4.

and B29 & B28 from Trench to Guid line running E & W. from B28 Central to B29 Central. This Objective will be taken by D. & B. Coys.

5. D. Coy will form Defensive Flank facing Southwards in Trench running E & W. through H4.

6. The Second Objective will be a line from Trench at H5.a.3.5 to Trench at B24.d.5.4. thence along Trench to B29.a.5.4. C & A Coys will take this Objective leapfrogging through A & B Coys.

7. Dividing line Method of attack will be in

accordance with orders
given verbally to Coy. Commdr.

8. Barrage will commence
400 yards in front of forming
up position where it will
rest for 10 minutes. It will
then advance by 100 yards
lifts every 3 minutes.
Halt of 10 minutes will be
made at first objective.
It will proceed to final
objective in two lifts
resting 17 minutes after
1st lift. After 2nd lift
a protective barrage will
be placed. Trench on left
Coy. objective will be
dealt with specially.

9. Bn HQ will be S.6.6.
Coys. HQ will be at

advanced as quickly as
possible.

10. Advanced Report Post
will be established at
H.2.b.8.8.

11. R.A.P. will be at
9.6.b.8.7.

(Sgd) F. Brook.
26.8.18   Lieut-Col
                Comdg. The Hunts Rgt.

Secret.

ORIGINAL
Vol 4

T.15
Michaels

War Diary.
2/4th. Battn. Hampshire Regt.

From SEPTEMBER 1st 1918
To SEPTEMBER 30th 1918

J Bayrk
Lt. Colonel.
Commanding 2/4 Hampshire Regt.

ORIGINAL

2/4th Stafford Reg

Army Form C. 2118.

WAR DIARY
or
INTELLIGENCE SUMMARY.
(Erase heading not required.)

Place	Date	Hour	Summary of Events and Information	Remarks and references to Appendices
	Sept 1			
	2		The Battalion remained in the area E. of SAPIGNIES and BEHAGNIES to which it had moved on being relieved by the 2/4 D. of W's Regt. on the night 29/30 of August.	
	3		Positions relatively the same this day, B, C, D Companies moving slightly forward to a position in trenches along the ridge. The Batt'n was relieved at dusk by troops of the 3rd Division (S. Staffs), and withdrew to bivouacs on railway N. of Courcelles	D.R.O. 2/9/18
			Casualties during these operations:—
			Lt. (A/capt.) J.F. BENNETT and 19 other ranks killed
			2Lt. C.B. RICHMOND (remained at duty), 2Lt. F.C. HOLBROOK and 121 other ranks wounded.
			2 O.R's missing
			The following awards were made for Gallantry during these operations.
			MILITARY MEDAL
			200343 C.S.M. Tildon J.H. 8470 Pte. Purdue W.
			201152 Sgt.(A/CQMS) Berry A.E. 33560 " Tonkim F.
			308830 Sgt. Patemore G. 25199 " Kidding A.E.
			8798 " Beltropp G.
			200316 Cpl. Huxon H.
			42296 Pte. Ford V.
			202475 " Guest G.H.
			356834 " Mersom F.
			210309 " Brandon S.
			200757 " Ellis J.
			202461 " Clarke F.W.
			201652 " Berring C.J.
			201825 " West P.
			202915 " Tappendin F.
			202428 " Street A.G.

ORIGINAL 1/4 Hants Regt

WAR DIARY or INTELLIGENCE SUMMARY

Army Form C. 2118.

(Erase heading not required.)

Place	Date	Hour	Summary of Events and Information	Remarks and references to Appendices
	Sept 4th		The Battalion remained in Bivouac area in Railway Cutting N. of Crenville till Sept 10th.	
			2.Lt. R.P. FENN rejoined Battn from Leave	A
			2.Lt. F.C. ISMAIL " " "	
			2.Lt. W.G. YOUNGS, E.B. PRATT, G.P. WHEELER joined the Battn.	A
	8th		The Battn took part in a Ceremonial Parade of the 186th Inf. Bde., including distribution of Medal Ribbons by Maj. Gen Sir R.D. WHIGHAM, G.O.C. 62nd Div. and a March-Past. Medal Ribbons were handed to the under-mentioned on this parade.	
			MILITARY CROSS.	
			2.Lt. (A/Capt.) R.P. FENN.	
			2.Lt. S.D. GREENHALGH.	
			MILITARY MEDAL	
			201109 CSM CHURCHER H.T.	
			1285 Sgt. JARVIS C.	
			250100 " MEADEN G.	
			260534 " DIGWEED J.R.	
			13714 Cpl. LANGSTON G.	
			205642 " CHARLTON T.	
			12334 " CHILDS F.	
			201562 " ALLEN F.J.	
			202440 " KENT R.A.	
			17079 Pte. RAYBOULD T.	
			31737 " BUNN J.	
			202848 " HILLIER J.	
			205440 " BUCKETT W.	

WAR DIARY or INTELLIGENCE SUMMARY

Army Form C. 2118.

ORIGINAL — 2/4 Hunts. Regt.

Instructions regarding War Diaries and Intelligence Summaries are contained in F. S. Regs., Part II. and the Staff Manual respectively. Title pages will be prepared in manuscript.

(Erase heading not required.)

Place	Date	Hour	Summary of Events and Information	Remarks and references to Appendices
	Sept 10th		The Battalion marched from railway, near Courcelles via Achiet-le-Grand, Bapaume, Baucourt, Hoplincourt, Bertincourt, Ruyaulcourt to bivouacs in S.W. corner of Havrincourt Wood, arriving there about 11 p.m. Transport lines established near Ruyaulcourt.	Ref Maps 1/2 57.C. NE. 57.C. SE. 1/20,000 — 2A
	11th		The Battalion remained in bivouac; a reconnaissance being made of the assembly positions	Appendix I. M. Operation Order 5th HCH 2 Brigade 190 PC Army. 27-9-18 Sheet 2/Hinmfell Map Appendix II. 11-9-18 Alexandra II Narrative of Operations 17-9-18 to 17-10-18
	12th	1 a.m.	The Battalion moved forward at 1 A.m. to assembly positions which were taken up by 3 A.m. These positions lay between Banbury Hill and Hubert Avenue, about Q 2 C, Battalion Headquarters being in K 32 C (junction of Hubert Avenue and Shropshire Reserve.	
		Zero 5.25 A.m.	The Battalion advanced to the attack on a 3-Company front; A Coy on the right, C in the centre and D on the left, with B Coy in support; each Company moving on a 1-platoon front.	
		5.45 A.m.	The complicated nature of the barrage made the attacking movement a difficult one; the defences of Havrincourt forbidding a frontal attack, so that attacking troops had to approach the village on their left, and then swing to their right.	
			The general scheme was to gain possession of Havrincourt, the first objective being a line passing through it from NE to SW, the final a line forward of the village to the NE.	⨉

Army Form C. 2118.

ORIGINAL 2/4 Hants. R.gt.

WAR DIARY
or
INTELLIGENCE SUMMARY.

(Erase heading not required.)

Instructions regarding War Diaries and Intelligence Summaries are contained in F. S. Regs., Part II. and the Staff Manual respectively. Title pages will be prepared in manuscript.

Place	Date	Hour	Summary of Events and Information	Remarks and references to Appendices
	12th	5.45 a.m.	The Battalion suffered several casualties before leaving their assembly positions at Zero and 20, an enemy barrage dropped almost as they started; but few further casualties were encountered until the S.W. corner of Havrincourt was approached, when fire was opened from about the S.W. corner of the village square. 36 prisoners were captured in East Avenue.	
		6.35 a.m.	On approaching the village the Battalion swung to the right, and at Zero and 70 was formed up at the S.W. of the village waiting for our barrage to lift. A.C. & D. Companies to whom was allotted the first objective, attacked on a 1- platoon frontage, two platoons to take the first half of the village, the remaining two platoons leap-frogging through to the Eastern edge.	
		7-0 a.m.	Shells from our barrage were still falling at Zero and 120, D Coy suffering several casualties in the Square.	
		7.28 a.m.	A.Co. captured the Chateau without much opposition but a little later were attacked by machine-gun fire. The guns were, however, successfully dealt with; 1 officer and 12 men with the M.Gs being taken; and 1 officer and several men killed.	
		8.30.	Shortly afterwards O.C. "A" Co. received information that two enemy M.Gs were holding up the attack of the 2/4 D. of W. Regiment, on the right, and moved a	

Army Form C. 2118.

WAR DIARY
or
INTELLIGENCE SUMMARY.

2/4" Hants. Regt.

ORIGINAL

(Erase heading not required.)

Instructions regarding War Diaries and Intelligence Summaries are contained in F. S. Regs., Part II. and the Staff Manual respectively. Title pages will be prepared in manuscript.

Place	Date	Hour	Summary of Events and Information	Remarks and references to Appendices
	12th		platoon to his right engaging the M.Gs, and succeeding in killing or capturing the crews of both guns. On the barrage lifting, A.C. & D. Companies went forward through the village clearing cellars and dug-outs, and taking a number of prisoners. C Coy met with some opposition near the Church, and had considerable fighting to do to be occupying its objective. D Coy on the left were held up by two M.Gs. but these were presently engaged, and the crews killed or captured.	B
		9.0. am	At this point B.G. phoned have come through the other companies and taken the final objective. The company had however lost heavily in the advance, and were unable to reach their jumping-off place before the barrage had gone forward. They thus lost the advantage of it and were held up eventually reinforcing the other two companies along the railway cutting, and E edge of the village.	
		11.30 am	The general position was then as follows:- D Coy held posts about K22. C31. (to the N of the village,) the remaining Companies held a line from that point southwards, C. Coy covering the S.E. corner of the village.	

ORIGINAL

WAR DIARY
INTELLIGENCE SUMMARY.

2/4 Hants. Regt.

Army Form C. 2118.

Place	Date	Hour	Summary of Events and Information	Remarks and references to Appendices
	12th		Company Headquarters and 1 platoon of C in support at K 27-672; 1 Platoon of C in reserve at K 27 d 79. Several posts were pushed forward of the railway line and about dusk reported enemy massing in T Wood. An attack was delivered about 7pm but was broken by our rifle and Lewis gun fire, and the enemy dispersed by the 18 pdr barrage.	7B
	Sept 12th/13th		The Battalion was relieved by the 5th Battalion K.O.Y.L.I., and went into reserve in SHROPSHIRE TRENCH. In the morning it was found that the posts of the S.E. of the village, amounting to between 50 and 60 men, chiefly of "A"C, had not been relieved. During the night the enemy worked forward along the Railway to the left Battn Sector, and got in rear of our posts enfilading the Railway. After some sharp fighting, these posts had to withdraw slightly, forming a defensive flank for the 2/4 D. of W. Regiment. About 6.30pm the 2/4 D. of W. took over the position and the party left behind then rejoined the Battalion in Shropshire Trench. Casualties during the 12th: 2/Lt H. BRYANT, and 27 O'Rs killed; 2/Lt H.S. WEEKS, 2/Lt W.J. WILSON, 2/Lt G.O.B. Visct UFFINGTON, 2/Lt C.A. GADSBY, 2/Lt F.C. ISAACS, 2/Lt E.B. PRATT, and 198 ORs wounded.	7B 7B

ORIGINAL

Army Form C. 2118.

WAR DIARY or INTELLIGENCE SUMMARY.

2/4" Hants. Regt.

(Erase heading not required.)

Instructions regarding War Diaries and Intelligence Summaries are contained in F.S. Regs., Part II and the Staff Manual respectively. Title pages will be prepared in manuscript.

Place	Date	Hour	Summary of Events and Information	Remarks and references to Appendices
	13th.	6.30 p.m.	Some shelling was experienced during the 13th in SHROPSHIRE TRENCH and near Bn: Headquarters. The latter moved back a short distance in the afternoon, to a position near CLAYTON CROSS, "A" Co: being with Headquarters in Reserve. Casualties on 13th: CAPTAIN C.P. BULLEY. and 4 OR's wounded.	
	14th.		The Battalion remained in the same positions during this day, except for a part of Melling the day was fairly quiet. Casualties during day :- 2 OR's killed. 5 OR's wounded.	
	15th.		The Battalion received orders to move at dusk, and marched to BEUGNY, and spent the night in bivouacs there.	
	16th.		The Battalion continued the march in the afternoon, stopping in a position on Railway cutting near Gomiecourt. Total casualties during these operations :- Killed :- 1 Officer 31 other ranks. Died of wounds :- 6 other ranks. Wounded :- 7 Officers 207 other ranks. Missing :- 38 other ranks.	

WAR DIARY ORIGINAL. Army Form C. 2118.
or
INTELLIGENCE SUMMARY. 2/4th Hants. Regt.
(Erase heading not required.)

Place	Date	Hour	Summary of Events and Information	Remarks and references to Appendices
	17th		Captain H.C.B. Cottam - 2/Lt C.B. Richmond - returned from leave.	JB
	18th		Lt. H. Brown - returned from leave.	JB
	20th		The Battalion remained in bivouac by Railway cutting near GOMICOURT till Sep 24th	JB
	24th		The Battalion took part in Brigade Inter-company Sports	JB
	25th		The Battalion left bivouac on the afternoon of Sept 25th and marched to BEUGNÂTRE where the night was spent, the 186 Inf: Brigade being under orders to take part in the general offensive about to be begun in the direction of CAMBRAI.	JB
	26th		The movement was continued at dusk on the 26th, a bivouac area being occupied east of BEAUMETZ-LES-CAMBRAI.	JB
	27th		On the morning of the 27th, the Battalion moved forward again, proceeding by HAVRINCOURT WOOD across the canal to a position just S.W. of HAVRINCOURT VILLAGE. The companies took up a position facing N.E. and remaining there for the day. Some shelling was experienced about dusk, but no casualties were suffered. In the evening the Battalion moved through HAVRINCOURT and spent the night in bivouac in the HINDENBURG LINE. (K-16.D.)	JB

F.M? Lieut Col
Comg 2/4 Hants Regt.

No 1

Operation Orders by Lieut. Col. F. Brook Drone
Comdg. 2/4 Hants Regt

11.9.18

Ref. 57 c S.E. 1/20000
57 c N.E. 1/20000

① The attack on HAVRINCOURT is being carried out by 18 Bde on left & 187 Infty Bde on right.

2ter

② Brigade boundaries after Zero to as follows:-
K 32 d. 9. 0 to K 33 c. 9. 8 thence main HAVRINCOURT — GRAINCOURT Rd to K. 22. c. 3. 1

③ Bde First Objective SHROPSHIRE SPUR Rd as far north as trench junction K.34 a. 9. 3 thence to S.E. corner of HAVRINCOURT thence along Eastern edge of village to K.22 C.4.1

(3) cont: Second Objective. Sunk Rd K.34.c.4.9.
— trench junction K.35.a.9.9. — trench
junction K.29.c.7 & thence along
KIMBER TRENCH to the CHAPEL at K.22.d.2.4

(4) First Objective will be captured by 5 D.L.I.
on the right, 9/ D.L.I. in the centre,
2/4 Hants (less one Coy) on the left.

(5) Second Objective will be captured by the
9/ D.L.I. on the right and one Coy 2/4 Hants
on the left.

(6) Inter Battn Boundary between 2/4 Hants &
9/ D.L.I. will be :- Road Junction
at K.27.d.4.7 to South East corner
of HAVRINCOURT VILLAGE.
Between 2/4 Hants and 9 D.L.I. :- K.28.a.6.0
— T Wood (inclusive).
Between 2/4 Hants & 5 K.O.Y.L.I. Main
HAVRINCOURT – GRAINCOURT Rd.

(a) Coy between 2/4 Hants & 2/4 Kings L.I.
Railway from K 22 C.3.2 to CHAPEL

(B) The Battn will attack 1st Objective on a
three Coy front, each Coy attacking on
a platoon front.
A Coy on the right
C Coy in centre
D Coy on Left.

(C) The Battn 2nd Objective will be taken
by B Coy who will attack on a three
platoon frontage with one platoon
in reserve. This Coy will leap
frog through the other Coys at
Eastern side of the village.

(D) Forming up place will be Q.2.c between
BANBURY HILL & HUBERT AVENUE
Coys will be in position at 3 am.

(10) The village will be divided as follows:-

A Coy ~~right~~ Southern edge of village to line running E & W immediately S of the CHURCH (Including the CHATEAU)

C Coy From A Coy northern boundary to road running from K 27 d 6 7 2 to K 28 a 6 7.

D Coy From C Coy's left to Battn left boundary (i.e. main HAVRINCOURT — GRAINCOURT Road)

(11) Battn Battle HQrs will be at Q 2 a 5 7.

(12) Advanced Report centre will be established at by C Coy Signallers at KNUT AVENUE.

(13) ~~Zero will be 5·25~~ Barrage table will be notified verbally to Company Commanders.

19.

(14). Zero will be 5.25 am
(15). Aid Post will be at Q2.c.3.3

F Brook Lieut Col

Orders issued at 10 am 11/9/18.

Op. Orders
12/9/18

Original.

SECRET.

War Diary.

2/4 Hampshire Regiment.

From :- 1-10-18.   To :- 31-10-18.

Vol: xvii.

T.16

J. Cockburn Major:
Commanding 2/4 Hants Regiment.

Original.

Army Form C. 2118.

WAR DIARY
or
INTELLIGENCE SUMMARY.
(Erase heading not required.)

2/4 Hampshire Regt

Place	Date	Hour	Summary of Events and Information	Remarks and references to Appendices
	Oct. 1st		[See Narrative of Operations appended to War Diary for September 1918]	Ref. Map. 57 C. 1/40000.
	2		The Battalion moved back to bivouac area N. of HAVRINCOURT (K 21 b 66)	Appendix I Narrative of Operations from Oct 19th – 22nd
	5th		Lt.Col. F. Brook DSO. MC. proceeded on leave to UK. Capt. A.F.L. Bacon proceeded on leave to UK. Maj. R.M. Titmarsh assumed Command of the Battn., vice Lt.Col. Brook, on leave.	Appendix II 2/4 Hampshire Regt Order No II
	6th		Lt.-Qmr. S.A. Thomson rejoined the Battalion from leave. 2Lt. H.F. Wheeler, 2Lt. Mill, 2Lt. King joined the Battalion on posting, from U.K.	RDT
	7th		Received Warning Order to move.	RDT
	8th		The Battalion marched at dusk, proceeding through HAVRINCOURT and FLESQUIERES to bivouac area in L19 b 53 (about), and remained there throughout the night.	RDT
	9th		The Battalion moved about 1400 hrs through MARCOING to RUMILLY, and spent the night in billets there (G 15 a 3.2).	RDT
	10th		The Battalion moved about 1500 hrs. and proceeded to SERANVILLERS, and spent the night in billets there (H 19 d. 9.6).	RDT
	11th		The Battalion moved at 1000 hrs., and proceeded via WAMBAIX and ESTOURMEL to CARNIERES, and spent the night in billets there (C 13 d.9.6). 2Lt. A.C. Mathew rejoined from hospital and was taken on Hdqrs. Coy.	RDT
	12th		The Battalion remained at CARNIERES. 2Lt. Wiltshire rejoined from leave. 2Lt. Bolwell joined the Battalion on posting, from U.K.	RDT

Original

Army Form C. 2118.

WAR DIARY
or
INTELLIGENCE SUMMARY.
(Erase heading not required.)

2/4 Hampshire Regt:

Place	Date	Hour	Summary of Events and Information	Remarks and references to Appendices
	Oct. 13th		The Battalion moved about 1530 hrs, and proceeded to BOUSSIERES.	RAP
	14th		At BOUSSIERES. Maj. R.M.Tidmarsh was evacuated to hospital, Maj. Parsons taking over Command of the Battalion.	RAP
	15th		At BOUSSIERES. Maj. G.E.C. Cockburn DSO. MC. Royal Irish Fusiliers, assumed Command of the Battalion, vice Maj. R.M.Tidmarsh to hospital. 2 Lt. Gadsby returned from hospital and proceeded on leave to U.K.	RAP
	16th		At BOUSSIERES.	RAP
	17th		The Battalion moved at 1430 hrs, and proceeded via BEVILLERS to QUIEVY, remaining in billets there till the night of the 19th.	RAP
	19th 20th 21st 22nd		For Operations from Oct 19th - 21st incl. see Appendix I & Appendix II.	Appendix I Narrative of Operations from Oct 19th - 22nd Appendix II 2/4 Hampshire Regt Order No III
	22nd		The Battalion proceeded to Billets in BEVILLERS, arriving about 2000 hours.	RAP
	23rd / 30th		The Battalion remained at BEVILLERS, and carried out training in that area till Oct 30th inclusive.	RAP
	31st		The Battalion moved to SOLESMES.	RAP

G. Cockburn Major
Commanding 2/4 Bn. Hampshire Regt.

Ref. Maps. 57 B NE 1/20000
51 A SE 1/20000

Appendix I

2-4th Hampshire Regiment.
Narrative of Operations from 19th October 1918 to 22nd October 1918.

---oOo---

Oct. 19th

On the night of the 19th October 1918 the Battalion moved to a preliminary assembly position in a cutting in the St. VAAST - St. PYTHON railway, about half a mile from St. PYTHON. This was completed by 2330 hours without undue difficulty; though there was a certain amount of stray shelling, only one casualty was incurred en route.

20th

At 0050 hours on the 20th October 1918 the Battalion moved up to its final assembly position between the N of St. PYTHON and the village of St. PYTHON in rear of the 5th Duke of Wellington's, companies being disposed from N. to S. in the following order - A, D, B, C. There was a certain amount of intermittent rifle, M.G. and Shell fire, but this move was completed by 0115 without any casualties. Battalion Headquarters remaining in the cutting. Zero hour was at 0200. The 5th Duke of Wellington's had already crossed the river SELLE by Zero hour, so at Zero hour the leading companies crossed the river by the bridge erected in the village and re-organised on the Eastern bank; this move was completed by 0230 hours without any casualties. C Coy, who were responsible for the mopping up of the centre of the village of SOLESMES, did not cross till 0300 hours. The very greatest credit is due to 2/Lieut. S.D. Greenhalgh M.C., who, with two observers and two runners, was responsible for guiding the companies from their preliminary positions to their final assembly positions and directing the companies across the river SELLE. Although badly gassed, in reconnoitring the ground prior to the companies moving up, he carried on under fire with the greatest coolness and sound judgement, the complete success of this preliminary operation being solely due to this Officer, who by his tireless energy set a magnificent example to the Battalion.

The weather conditions were very bad, torrents of rain and no moon, though it was still possible to see for a distance of about twenty yards, this lack of bright moonlight proved rather an advantage during the preliminary movements; but rather a disadvantage during the final operation of forming posts and mopping up the village of SOLESMES.

Company objectives were as follows :-

A. Company. one platoon strong point in D.6.d.4.7.
one " " " " E.1.c.1.2.
one platoon mopping up between strong points above and road in D.6.d.6.8. - E.1.c.6.

D. Company. one platoon in strong point in D.6.b.9.1.
one " " " " E.1.c.4.7.
one platoon to mop up between above strong points and road in D.6.d.6.8. - E.1.c.1.6.

B. Company. one platoon in strong point in E.1.a.8.8.
one " " " " E.1.a.9.1.
one platoon to mop up between above strong points and road in D.6.b.9.1. & E.1.c.4.8.
E.1.c.4.8.

C. Company. one platoon to mop up area between road in E.1.c.1.2. - E.1.c.4.8. and road in E.1.c.6.3. - E.1.c.5.7.
one platoon to mop up area on right of road in E.1.c.6.3. - E.1.c.5.7. along road to E.1.c.8.2.

A. Company, on reforming on the Eastern bank of the river proceeded along the St. PYTHON - SOLESMES road were temporarily delayed owing to the houses in St. PYTHON not having been completely mopped up. This completed, they passed through the

5th D.of W. and continued their advance, but met with very heavy rifle and M.G. fire from the outskirts of SOLESMES, this opposition was eventually overcome, two machine guns and about thirty prisoners being captured. The first post was then established by the leading platoon in D.1.d.4.7. about 0430 hours without further opposition. The second platoon, passing through the first post, met with considerable machine gun fire, but were able to push on, capturing two more machine guns and about twenty prisoners, establishing their post in E.1.c.1.2. about 0515 hours. The third platoon then carried on mopping up the area allotted to them.

D. Company skirting the houses of ST.PYTHON, leap-frogged a company of the 5th D of W in the road about D.6.b.2.3. and advanced on their objectives, but were met with heavy machine gun fire from behind a loop-holed brick wall immediately to their front, also from enfilade machine gun fire from their right flank. This considerably delayed their progress, but by an outflanking movement one machine gun was captured, the other being driven into the town and eventually surrendering to the 2/4th Y and L.Regiment who were approaching the town from the opposite direction. Posts were then established with little further opposition, the leading platoon at D.6.b.9.1., the second platoon at E.1.c.4.7. by 0530 hours; the third platoon carrying on mopping up the area allotted to them.

B. Company, following close behind D Company, made straight for their first objective, passing through a company of the 5th D of W about E.1.a.1.5. and established a post at E.1.c.8.8. with little opposition about 0530. The second platoon advancing on the right of the first platoon met with considerable resistance from Machine gun fire and a Trench mortar firing from about E.1.c.4.7. The opposition was overcome with rifle grenades and Lewis gun fire and a post was established at E.1.a.9.1. about 0615 hours, the third platoon carrying on mopping up.

C Company, crossing the river SELLE at 0300 hours, advanced along the St.PYTHON - SOLESMES road through the two posts formed by A Company, and mopped up the area allotted to them with little opposition. The third platoon of this company were kept in reserve about D.6.c.6.4. This company captured five machine guns and two Tench Mortars without a single caualty.

The Battalion finally completed its objectives by 0715 hours

Battalion Headquarters moved up from the cutting enbankment to a house in St.PYTHON about V.2.9.d.9.8. at 0315 hours, establishing a forward report centre a D.6.c.7.2. under the command of Major B.E.T.Parsons, who rendered very valuable assistance throughout the operations.

SOLESMES was heavily shelled from 0400 till about 1000 hours when shelling slackened. Units of the 185 Brigade leap-frogged the post at E.1.a.8.8. about 0830 and continued the advance The Battalion then re-organised, each platoon post already formed being held, with the third platoon of each company in support. C.Company were held in reserve about the Town Hall in SOLESMES. Intermittent heavy shelling continued throughout the day and night until about 0900 hours on the morning of the 21st.

Touch was maintained as soon as established throughout operations with the 5th D of W on the left and the 2/4th Yorks and Lancs on the right.

21st. During the morning of the 21st orders were received from Brigade to relieve the company of the 2/4th Yorks and Lancs occupying the SOLESMES line; relief was completed by 1430 hours, companies being disposed as follows, B and D Companies remained in their positions. C Company relieved the posts established by the 2/4th Yorks and Lancs in E.1.d.2.9. - E.1.d.5.4. - E.1.d.9.4. A Company moving up to Billets about E.1.d.o.5. Battalion Headquarters were located at E.1.c.8.6. The situation remained unchanged except for intermittent shelling until the Battalion was relieved by units of

22nd. the 3rd Division at 1730 hours on the 22nd inst. On relief the Battalion proceede to Billets in BEVILLERS arriving by 2000 hours.

Total Casualties

Total Captures during Operations :-

    8   Machine Guns.
    6   Trench Mortars.
  262 Prisoners.

Total Casualties :-

Officers.		Other Ranks.		
Killed.	Wounded.	Killed.	Wounded.	Died of Wounds
NIL	1	7	17	1

90% of the Casualties were incurred from Hostile Shell fire, and not from the actual Attack and Capture of the Objectives.

The following point was brought out during Operations and proved very successful. Platoons detailed to Mop up did not carry Lewis Guns, this improved the Mopping up Strength of the platoons, and saved the Guns unnecessary exposure.
These Guns were sent up to Companies as soon as all Objectives had been taken.
No Lewis Guns were lost during Operations.

26-10-1918.   Commanding 2/4th Battn. Hampshire Regiment. Major,

I.

2/4 Hampshire Regiment.
Operation Order. No. II.

Appendix II

Reference Map: 57 B. N.E. 1/2000.
51 A.S.E.

1. The 186. Infantry Brigade, to which is attached the 2/4 Battn. Yorks and Lancs Regiment, will capture the town of SOLESMES, and the line of the first objectives from E 76.9.0 to W 25.6.2.3. on Zero Day, at an hour to be notified later.

2. The 2/4 Yorks. Regiment are attacking from the south, and the platoon of B Company 2/4 Hants, forming No. 6. Post, will get into touch with No. 12. Post, formed by D Coy - 2/4 Yorks. Regiment, as soon as possible after the post's formation.

3. The 5th D of Ws are attacking on the north of the 2/4 Hants Regt.

4. The 2/4 D of W. will attack the railway line between the river D 12 d. 9.8. and ravine in D 5 d 8.2.

5. The 185 Infantry Brigade will pass through the 186 Inf: Bde, at about Zero and 300 minutes, and will capture the final objective.

6. Order of march :- Hdqrs - A, D, B, C.
Signal limber and M.E. Cart will move in rear of Headquarters; Lewis-gun mules will move in rear of platoons to which Lewis-guns belong.
Ammunition - mules in rear of rear platoons of each Coy.

7. Route :- Present billets in QUIEVY. - cross-roads D 14. C.3.1. cross-roads D 8.b.4.7. - road-junction about D.2.d.56 - road-junction D.3.a.8.6. - along main ST. VAAST — ST. PYTHON road, to a point about D 4 d 6.9. - thence across country to a point in railway cutting D 5. a 1.7. In order to assist Companies, guides will be placed at the following points :- D 2 d. 5.6. and D 4 d 6.9. On arrival in the cutting, Companies will be situated from S.E. to N.W. in the order, A. D. B. C.
10 minutes between Companies - 40 yds between platoons -

II.

Continued:—

In the event of heavy hostile shelling, Company Commanders, at their own discretion, will dispose their platoons to meet the situation.

8. <u>Starting-point</u>:— cross-roads D 14 . C . 3 . 1.
Headquarters and Companies will pass at the following times:—

| Hdqrs. | A. | D. | B. | C. |
| 2130 hours. | 2200 hrs. | 2210 hrs. | 2220 hrs. | 2230 hrs. |

9. <u>Battle Headquarters</u>, and R.A.P., will be located in Railway cutting, about D 5 a . 2 . 8. at Zero hour.
At Zero and 60 minutes, Battle Hdqrs and R.A.P. will move up to a house in ST. PYTHON, in V 30 . a . 2 . 8, and form a joint headquarters with 5th D. of W. Regiment.
Batt'n R.C. at D 6 a . 7 . 1. will be formed as soon as possible.

10. <u>Prior to Zero hour</u>, the Battalion will form up east of the HAUSSY—ST. PYTHON railway, just west of ST. PYTHON in V-29.d. Guides will be provided to take companies from railway cutting to forming-up positions. A. D. B. Companies will move off, and cross the river, as soon as the 5th. D of W. Regiment are clear; only one company crossing the river at a time. "C" Coy will not move until ordered.

11. <u>Objectives, and "mopping-up" areas</u>:—
"A" Company. objective. 1 platoon in D 6 . d . 4 . 7. } strong
                        1   "   " E 1 . C . 1 . 2. } points.
Mopping-up area:— between strong points, as above, and road in D 6 . d . 6 . 8. and E 1 . c . 1 . 6.

12. "D" Company.   1 platoon in strong point D 6 b 9 . 1.
                            1   "   "   "   "   E 1 c 4 . 7.
1 platoon to "mop-up" between above points and road in D 6 d . 6 . 8 — and E . 1 . c . 1 . 6.

Continued :-

III.

13. "B" Company.   1 platoon in strong point E.1.a.8.8.
                   1   "   "   "   " E.1.a.9.1.
   1 platoon to "mop up" between above points and road in
   D.6.b.9.1; and E.1.c.4.8.

14. "C" Company.   1 platoon to "mop up" area in :-
       between road in E.1.c.1.2 — E.1.c.4.8.
       and road in   E.1.c.6.3 — E.1.c.5.7.

               1 platoon to "mop up" area on right
   of road in E.1.c.6.3, E.1.c.5.7; along road to
   E.1.c.8.2; and thence along road to point in E.1.c.9.8

               1 platoon in reserve.

15. Communications.

   1. An advanced R.C. (telephone) will be pushed
      forward from V.29.d.8.5, to about D.6.a.8.1.

   2. A flag will be placed in position to denote
      Advanced Headquarters.

   3. Two pigeons will be issued to "B" Coy.

16.   ACKNOWLEDGE.

                    (Signed.) R.P. Fenn. Capt. & Adjt.
   18/10/18.   2/4 Hampshire Regiment.

RP7

Copy of letter from Lt. Col. Brook, re 2/4th Hants.

Castle Blayney,
Co. Monaghan.

Oct. 13th, 1918.

Dear Colonel Cave,-

Your letter reached me in the middle of battle. Since then I have wanted a chance to thank you for it and the heartiness of your good wishes and congratulations. Of course I knew how keenly interested you were in the exploits of the Battalion apart from the fact that your Son was in it and I assure you we are all proud to have earned the high esteem of our Honorary Colonel. We all know how proud you are of the name the Battalion has made, and if you knew what the Battalion has done as I know it your pride would be even greater. I am intensely proud to command it and I feel there is no better Unit in France. Prior to this I commanded the 2/5th West Riding Regt. That was a fine Battalion and when it was broken up or rather merged into the First Line I felt it most deeply. To have got my present command is more than recompense.

Some time ago I got your address from your Son and hoped to see you when I was on leave. You will see that I am now at home and expect to be in London next week (I attend an investiture on the 24th). I will send you word to your club when I get to town for I know you will be glad to learn more fully of the Battalion and of your Son. May I just say that your Son is one of my right hand men and if ever a father had justification for pride in his Son you have. He has done most magnificently and I am very hopeful that it will be recognized. He was fit and well when I left, like most of us he was a little tired, but I sent him off to the coast for a month's course so he will get his rest.

With kindest regards,

Yours sincerely,

(signed)   F. Brock,
Lieut.-Col.
2/4th Hants. Regt.

2/4th Battn. Hampshire Regiment.

NARRATIVE of Operations from 27th Septr. to 1st.
October 1918.

On the night of 26th September 1918 the Battalion moved to assembly positions S.W. of BEAUMETZ. Zero Hour was 5.20 a.m. 27th Septr. 1918 and the Battalion was due to cross the starting point at 6.20 p.m., This was done without difficulty and the Battalion was in position in SHROPSHIRE and CHEETHAM SUPPORT by 9.0 a.m; at 10.0 a.m. the Battalion moved forward to position S.W. of HAVRINCOURT and although there was a considerable amount of enemy shelling no casualties were sustained.

At 5.30 p.m. orders were received to move to K 16 a. As soon as the Battalion began to move HAVRINCOURT was heavily shelled and it was necessary to wait some time, the position allotted however was reached without casualties and the Commanding Officer then proceeded to Brigade for orders. The following were the orders received :-

5th D. of W. Regt. would form up in KAISER TRENCH N. of Railway and attack the village of MARCOING.

2/4th Hants Regt. Form up on the FLESQUIERES -RIBECOURT Road L 19 c., and follow the 5th D. of W. Regt. force the crossings over the Canal and establish a bridge-head extending from about CHATEAUT ALMA Lock to the Canal W. of MASNIERES.

2/4th D. of W. Regt. in Brigade Reserve ready to come through and exploit success gained Zero Hour fixed at 6.30 a.m.

At 4.0 a.m. the Battalion moved off to proceed to forming up position and the Commanding Officer reported to Brigade where he was informed that the Battalion might be required to attack MARCOING should the 5th D. of W. Regt. fail to reach forming up position by Zero Hour. Alternative orders to provide for both eventualities were given to the Companies on the forming up position.

The Companies were organised into three Platoons and were formed up as follows :-
"A" on Right
"C" on Left

These two Companies attacked on a two platoon frontage with one platoon in support their objective being the system of Trenches immediately W. of MARCOING.
"B" on Right
"D" on Left

These two Companies attacked on a one Platoon frontage they were to leap-frog through "A" and "C" Companies, fight their way through the village and establish posts on the Western edge of the Canal pushing posts to the Eastern Side at the bridges.

The advance was commenced promptly at Zero and as it was found that the 5th D. of W. Regt., had not arrived in position the Battalion pushed on with all speed after the barrage which was over-taken about L 21 a&c.

The enemy's Counter barrage was light and proved no hindrance, very few casualties being caused. The right forward Company got into line with the 18th. Brigade which was attacking on the right. Near DAGO TRENCH this Company saw an enemy battery of three guns the horses for which were just being rushed up, Lewis Gun fire was at once brought to bear on the gun positions and the gunners made off, some horses fell into our hands and some were killed by our barrage.   At this point the Company came under long range Machine Gun fire from our right, this was dealt with by the Hallamshires.

On the right of the MARCOING Road 11 prisoners and several Trench Mortars and Machine Guns were captured, the house at L 21 d.5.9. was held and after a sharp fight 9 prisoners with some Machine Guns were taken, this Company reached its objective without much further trouble except from Machine Gun fire from the Western edge of the Village, several more prisoners were taken in the neighbourhood of the road junction L 22 a.1.1.

The left Company reached PREMY SUPPORT L 21.a.3.2. without difficulty, beyond this enemy shelling including Gas was heavy there was very little Machine Gun fire except from the Village but an enemy Trench Mortar Battery was active from the Railway about L 22 c 4.5. this was put out of action by Lewis Gun fire; near PREMY TRENCH about L 22 a.0.9 an enemy field gun was captured with 10 prisoners. At this point there was some opposition from Machine Guns and rifles but these were silenced and several prisoners taken and the Company consolidated. We were not in touch with the Battalion on our left.

At this Stage "B" and "D" Companies leapfroged through having reached the first objective without any loss. The front Companies had driven in the enemy opposition from the W. edge of the Village and "B" Comapny got a footing in the Village without difficulty. On attempting to cross the ESCAUT RIVER they came under Machine Gun fire but two Lewis Guns of No. 5 Platoon quickly got superiority and the enemy gunners quickly fled one being killed. About L 22 b 3.0. another Machine Gun nest was encountered but the enemy on perceiving No 7. Platoon working round evacuated the position, the guns falling into our hands and three enemy wounded ~~falling into our hands~~. On approaching the the Canal considerable enemy Maching Gun and rifle fire was opened from the Railway E. of the Canal but after some difficulty this fire was overcome and post on the Eastern Bank of the Canal established, Capt. Cottam with a small party crossing the canal , the supporting Platoons of the Company did the mopping up and captured 10 prisoners.

The left Company had no difficulty in leapfrogging through "C" Company but came under heavy artillery fire about 300 yards W. of MARCOING ~~but~~ it quickly got a footing in the Village and one Platoon proceeded to work round the North West of the Village. Several prisoners surrendered. The crossing of the River ESCAUT L 17 c.1.1. heavy Machine Gun fire was encountered from buildings near and from CHATEAU TALMA but by means of Lewis Gun fire and rifle and supporting fire ~~fire~~ from a platoon of the 5th D. of W. Regt., who were working round the North Western edge of the Village, the opposition was driven out and the enemy fled across the Canal; considerable difficulty was experienced in establishing posts along the canal bank but this was eventually successful. Heavy fire was then brought to bear from all our posts and two Platoons of the 5th D. of W. Regt., who had reached the bank, on the enemy on the Eastern Side their fire was overcome and the D. of W. men crossed and established themselves on the Eastern side being subsequently followed by the remainder of the 5th D.of W Regt.

The Battalion was then re-organised the right forward Company holding the Canal Bank with two ~~posts~~ positions in six posts and one Platoon in support which also guarded the right flank.
The 187th. Brigade not being close up. The left forward Company had two platoons in five posts along the Canal left post being immediately N. of lock in L 17 d. with one platoon in support at L 23 a 5.9.

The right supporting Company had two platoons between the Railway and Road L 22.a & c. and one Platoon in support astride the road L 22 a.0.2.

The left Supporting Company detached one Platoon to guard the left flank of the Battalion at L 16.d.9.3. the remaining two

- 3 -

occupying trenches in L 22 a.

During the operations the following were captured :-

.... Prisoners

.... Machine Guns

.... Trench Mortars

.... Field Guns

At 5.0 p.m. on the 29th September 1918 verbal instructions were received from the Brigade Commander to move to RUMILLY TRENCH and from there attack the MASNIERES - CAMBRAI Road and the Village of RUMILLY at the same time information was received that a strong pocket of the enemy with Machine Guns had established itself in RUMILLY SUPPORT in G.14 c & d between the Companies of the 2/4th D. of W. Regt., our Barrage was to fall N. of RUMILLY SUPPORT from 6.0 to 6.30 p.m. after which it was to lift by stages to the Eastern side of RUMILLY.

The Battalion at once got on the move and orders given to the Company Commanders as follows :-

"A" and "B" Companies were to take the line of the MASNIERES-CAMBRAI road.

"C" and "D" Companies passing through and taking the village of RUMILLY.

If this could not be carried out orders were given that the line RUMILLY SUPPORT should be made good. While the Battalion was passing through MARCOING the enemy shelled the village heavily and "D" Company had several casualties but by 6.0 p.m. the Battalion began to cross the Canal. Owing to this having to be done in single file and steps and banks negotiated progress was necessarily slow and by the time the foreard Coys: approached RUMILLY TRENCH the barrage had gone and darkness was coming on. The right forward Company had crossed the Canal in L 23 d. and had reached RUMILLY TRENCH about G 20 a & b when it came under heavy Machine Gun. This Company could see nobody on either flank and it was impossible to advance further so the O.C. Company organised his Company in depth one Platoon in RUMILLY TRENCH and two Platoons in G 20.a.

Left Forward Company reached RUMILLY SUPPORT TRENCH in G 13.b & G.14. a. where it found "A" Company of the 2/4th D. of W. Regt., here the Company Commander was told that the 2nd. Division was not in advance of FLAT FARM and that strong enemy pocket was still in existence in RUMILLY SUPPORT, It was almost dark, nobody could be seen advancing on either flank so Capt. Cottam decided not to advance further.

Right supporting Company had difficulty owing to intense artillery fire in crossing the Canal and it was quite dark when the railway was reached. Lieut. Gotelee thereupon went into a dug-out, took the bearing from a map of the line of his advance, set his Compass and led the Company forward on a compass bearing and went straight to where A Company was and this Company reorganised in trenches S. of G. 18 a. & G 19 b.

The left supporting Company followed closely in rear of "B" Company and organised astride the railway in RUMILLY TRENCH with one Platoon in support.

Battalion Headquarters was established in MARCOING at L 23.a. 3.7.

The O.C. "B" Company sent a patrol at once to work down RUMILLY SUPPORT to endeavour to gain touch with the right

Companies of the 2/4th D. of W. Regt., but on reaching C.14.c.3.7. the patrol came under heavy Machine Gun fire the leader being killed, the patrol withdrawing.

Another Patrol worked to the left getting in touch with the 2nd. Division about G 13.b.5.5.

During the night "A" and "D" Companies which were in support were very heavily shelled several casualties being caused.

On the Morning of the 30th it was still found that the enemy was still holding the central portion of RUMILLY SUPPORT TRENCH and it was decided to make an effort to clear them out. One Platoon attacked from RUMILLY TRENCH about G 14 c.2.5. towards G 14 c.7.7. while one Platoon attacked along RUMILLY SUPPORT TRENCH from G 14.c.R.R.3.7. eastwards no artillery fire was available, and an effort was made to screen and cover the attack by smoke bombs and rifle grenades. The attempt was made at 11.45 a.m. The Platoon attacking from RUMILLY TRENCH came at once under annihilating Machine Gun fire and though Lt. Turner with great great gallantry succeeded in getting within 30 yards of the enemy position success was impossible, this Officer and most of the Platoon becoming casualties.

The other attacking Platoon pushed across our barrier and attempted to get along the trench to the enemy position but as the trench in this part was very shallow there was no cover from the enemy Machine Guns which completely enfiladed the trench Capt. Cottam and several of his men were killed and with great difficulty the remainder withdrew across our barrier.

Later on information was received from Brigade that the 185th Brigade intended to attack RUMILLY at 2.30 p.m. from the South and it was decided to make a further attack on the enemy pocket at the same time and a barrage was arranged but unfortunately it was impossible for it to fire on the sector of the RUMILLY SUPPORT TRENCH occupied by the enemy.

At 2.30 p.m. the attack was made again on similar lines to the former and this time the Platoon which attacked from RUMILLY TRENCH under 2/Lt. Shawland crawled forward through the long grass succeeded in getting across into the enemy sector at the same time the other Platoon dashed along the trench.

Several of the enemy made off towards the Railway and were engaged by our Lewis Guns several casualties being inflicted.. A great effort was made to push along the trench eastwards but again terrific Machine Gun fire was brought to bear directly on to our men from positions in RUMILLY SUPPORT and from the Building G 14 d.8.7. five of our men being killed and several wounded.

The position was quite unintenable and our men had to withdraw to our former position in RUMILLY SUPPORT. During the whole of the day our men were actively employed sniping and using Rifle Grenades on the enemy positions several enemy were seen to fall. "A" and "D" Companies which were in support were subjected to very heavy artillery fire and sustained heavy losses.

During the night instructions were received that the Suffolk Regt. would attack through us at dawn and at 5.0 a.m. our men were withdrawn from RUMILLY SUPPORT TRENCH as our barrage was to fall there.

"C" Company was ordered to detail a Platoon to rush along RUMILLY SUPPORT TRENCH and mop it up as soon as the Suffolks passed over, 2/Lt. Shawlands volunteered for this as also did his Platoon, Immediately the Barrage lifted off RUMILLY SUPPORT TRENCH and the first wave of the Suffolks had gone over, this party rushed along over the enemy barrier bombing the dugouts and killing any enemy met. Twenty two Machine Guns were counted in RUMILLY SUPPORT and Five in C.T. running towards the Railway 22 dead Bosche were counted and 70 prisoners taken.

Orders were then given for the Battalion to withdraw to HAVRINCOURT, this was carried out without further loss.

Total Captures during this part of the operations :-
  Machine Guns   26
  Converted Lewis Guns 4
  Prisoners   70

Total Casualties during operations :-
  Officers.   Other Ranks.
     3   88

The following points were brought out during these operations :-

1. The Brigade practice of having a sealed pattern type of formation for attack proved the salvation of the operations. Without this operations which were successfully carried out would have been impossible.

2. The Leap-frog method more than justified itself.

3. In Village attack a frontage of one Platoon per Company proved most satisfactory. Once The thrust has carried to the far edge of the village, the mopping up is easy.

4. The value of Rifle Grenades was again demonstrated.

5. The Battalion posted all signallers at Headquarters and sent these forward to establish stations as required. This worked very well and signaller casualties were avoided.

F. Brook
Lieut. Colonel.
Commanding 2/4th Battn Hampshire Regt.

SECRET   Vol. XVIII

ORIGINAL

WAR DIARY

- of -

2/4 HAMPSHIRE REGIMENT

From :- 1.11.18
to :- 30.11.18

T.17

F Brook
Commanding 2/4 Hampshire Regiment

Army Form C. 2118.
ORIGINAL

WAR DIARY
or
INTELLIGENCE SUMMARY.
(Erase heading not required.)

2/4 Hampshire Regiment

Vol XVIII. page 2.

Place	Date	Hour	Summary of Events and Information	Remarks and references to Appendices
	Nov. 25th		The Battalion moved by march route from DEVANT-LES-BOIS to ST. GERRARD.	RPT
	26th		The Battalion moved by march route from ST. GERRARD to EVREHAILLES, crossing the R. MEUSE at YVOIR.	RPT Ref. Map. MARCHE 9. 1/100,000.
	27th		The Battalion moved by march route from EVREHAILLES via PURNODE, DORINNE to area FAIYS - BARSENAL. Battⁿ Hdqs at the CHÂTEAU BARSENAL. and ACHÊNE	RPT
	27th - 30th		The Battalion remained in billet area as above.	RPT

J Booth Lieut Colonel
Commanding 2/4 Hampshire Regiment

2/4th BATTALION, HAMPSHIRE REGIMENT.

NARRATIVE OF OPERATIONS - 3RD TO 11TH NOVEMBER 1918.

Ref. Map Sheet 51 A. S.E. 20000.
1

On the night of the 2nd November 1918 the Battalion moved to RUESNES preparatory to carrying out an Attack on the morning of the 4th; here it was subjected to heavy Shell Fire. No casualties were sustained.

On the 3rd reconnaissance was carried out, and at 11.30 p.m. the Battalion proceeded to Assembly Position along Railway and Track in R.16.a. and d.. During the early part of the night, Tape had been laid by 2/Lieut. S.D.Greenhalgh, so no difficulty was experienced in reaching Point of Assembly. The Battalion arriving at 2.30 a.m. Disposition of Battalion as follows :-

    A. Company on the Right.   B. Company on the Left.
    C. Company Right Support.   D. Company Left Support.

While forming up, there was a considerable amount of Enemy Machine Gun and Shell Fire; but no casualties were incurred. The Battalion Attack was part of a large Attack along the whole Front - the New Zealanders attacking LE QUESNOY on our immediate Right - the 187th Infantry Brigade attacking ORSINVAL on our immediate Left. Each Company attacked on a three Platoon Frontage with one Platoon in Support. Battalion Headquarters was established at R.21.b.3.5.

A. & B. Companies had as their Objective the Ravine from R.17.d.5.0. to VIEUX MOULIN.

C. & D. Companies were to leap-frog through and take the High Ground along the LE QUESNOY - ORSINVAL Road, making the Liaison Posts on each Flank.

Zero was 5.30 a.m. and at that hour the Attack was launched. The Enemy Counter-Barrage came down at once along the Line of Railway, causing fairly heavy casualties; but the Companies without hesitation pushed forward.

A. Company met considerable opposition from Machine Gun fire, the Company Commander, Captain W. Brierley being wounded; but with fine dash they took their Objective with three Machine Guns and 55 Prisoners.

B. Company encountered an Enemy Strong Point almost at once in the Copse R.16.b. After a sharp fight the Enemy Machine Guns were silenced, the crews either killed or captured, and the Advance continued. The Ravine was strongly held but the resolute bearing of the Company beat down the opposition; - some Machine Guns, one Officer and about 80 Prisoners being captured.

C. and D. Companies were following close behind, and as the Barrage lifted, they leap-frogged through and advanced up the Slope. The Enemy held a very strong Position with many Machine Guns; but the men were keen for the Fight and the Platoons were handled so skilfully that the Position was carried. Sergt. Hamilton greatly distinguished himself at this Stage. At various positions on this Company Front, the Enemy fought well; but the opposition was soon overcome. Several Machine Guns and about 100 Prisoners being captured.

D. Company on the Left, had the same kind of opposition to encounter, the Enemy holding the Houses and Orchards strongly. Heavy Enemy Machine Gun and Trench Mortar fire was met; but this was subdued by the Lewis Gunners and the Objective reached, many Machine Guns, and 4 Trench Mortars and about 60 Prisoners being taken.

The Battalion was then re-organised and connection established with the New Zealanders and the 187th Infantry Brigade. At about 7.0 a.m. the 2/4th Duke of Wellington's Regt. passed the Battalion and continued the Attack. Battalion Headquarters was moved to R.17.b.8.8.

SHEET 2.

At 6.0.a.m. on the morning of the 5th the Battalion moved to HITONSART where it billetted for the night. During the night, orders were received that the Attack was to be continued, by 186th Infantry Brigade on the following morning, and the Battalion was ordered to move at 6.0 a.m. to N.10.c. and await Orders. At 8.30a.m. Orders were received to move to OBIES where the 185th Infantry Brigade was holding the Line and in conjunction with the 2/4th Duke of Wellington's Regt. capture the BROWN LINE (BAVAY - AVESNES Road) and if possible exploit this to DELHAYE WOOD. On OBIES being reached the situation was found to be obscure and the Battalion was halted while reconnaisance was being made. This reconnaisance was carried out by Major B.R.T.Parsons.

The disposition on forming up was as follows ;C. and A. Companies on the Road between O.7.c.6.4. and O.7.a.7.4.; D. and B. Companies along the Road running North and South through the E in MECQUIGNIES. No barrage was available, but the Battalion had the use of two Sections of Artillery for forward work and two Batteries for targets of opportunity. In addition to this, two Sections of Machine Guns were available. The Artillery was used at the start for putting Shrapnel Fire over the Villages of MECQUIGNIES, GOGNIAUX and LE TIMON.

At 11.30a.m. the Attack was launched; very little opposition being encountered although the whole Area was subjected to heavy Shell Fire. On approaching the Villages considerable difficulty arose on the Left Flank from Machine Guns in O.1.b.; these Guns firing into the backs of D. and B. Companies. It was found that the Guards who were operating on our Left were over 1000 yards behind, but the Attack pushed forward. Some opposition was met in GOGNIAUX but after sharp fighting in the Orchards the Machine Guns were captured; some Enemy killed and 4 Prisoners taken.

The Villages were the Objectives for C. and D. Companies and A. and B. Companies attempted to come through, but again heavy enfilade Machine Gun Fire from the Left made the Advance most difficult.

In the meantime 2/Lieut. H.L.Willsher pushing ahead forced the BROWN LINE at QUENE-AU-LOUP and drove the Enemy toward BOIS-DU-CHENE inflicting severe casualties. Although isolated and exposed to enfilade fire this party held on to its Position and so enabled A. and B. Companies to work forward on the Right Flank and these two Companies eventually succeeded in occupying the Road from QUENE-AU-LOUP to the CROSS ROADS O.3.2.6.9. driving the Enemy towards CONQUEVILLE. As the Guards were some distance behind on the Left, D. Company pushed forward - one Platoon to O.9.a.0.9. to protect the Left Flank.

Battalion Headquarters was at OBIES being subsequently moved to GOGNIAUX. The night passed quietly and at dawn the Attack was continued by 5th Duke of Wellingtons Regt and 2 Battalions of the 185th Infantry Brigade, this Battalion being responsible for guiding them to the BROWN LINE.

At 8.0. a.m. on the morning of the 7th, the Posts of the Battalion were withdrawn and the men billetted in adjoining houses. The Battalion remained at these billets until 6.0 a.m. on the morning of the 9th when it moved forward preparatory to continuing the Attack through the 187th Infantry Brigade on SOUS-LE-BOIS and LOUVROIL; P.14.d. being the Brigade rendezvous. It was then reported that the 187th Infantry Brigade was making good progress and that it was unlikely the Battalion would be required to Attack, and instructions were received to move at 1.30 p.m. to SOUS-LES-BOIS where the Battalion would billet for the night and take over the Line West of LOUVROIL and South of the RIVER SAMBRE early on the morning of the 10th. This was done. C. and D. Companies holding an Outpost Line along the RIVER West of ROUSIES from Q.17.d. - Q.5.d., with A. and B. Companies holding the High Ground Q.16.b. - Q.10.d. and b., Headquarters being at about Q.9.central.

At dawn on the morning of the 11th an Officers' Patrol under Captain R.H.Coteles advanced to RECQUIGNIES and HARPONT. No Enemy were discovered and a considerable quantity of Railway Stock fell into our hands.

At 9.0 a.m. Orders were received that Hostilities would cease at 11.0 a.m. the Armistice having been signed.

The Posts with the exception of those holding the River Crossings to Q.11.b.8.0. - Q.6.b.5.9. were then withdrawn,

SHEET 3.

these two Posts becoming Examining Posts.

CASUALTIES.

KILLED.		WOUNDED.		MISSING.	
OFFICERS.	O.R'S.	OFFICERS.	O.R'S.	OFFICERS.	O.R'S.
-	19.	2	70.	-	2

CAPTURES.

PRISONERS.		MACHINE GUNS.	TRENCH MORTARS.	
OFFICERS.	O.R'S.		HEAVY.	LIGHT.
3.	300.	15.	1.	5.

RP7

F. Brook.
Lieut. Colonel,
15th November 1918.   Commanding 2/4th Battn., Hampshire Regiment.

Secret.

Original
Vol 7

T.18
4 sheets

War Diary
of
2/4 Hampshire Regiment.
Volume 18.

From: December 1st 1918.
To: December 31st 1918.

F. Brough
Lieut-Colonel
Commanding 2/4 Hampshire Regiment.

2 - 1 - 1919.

Vol XVIII
Original
Army Form C. 2118.

WAR DIARY
or
INTELLIGENCE SUMMARY.
(Erase heading not required.)

2/4 Hampshire Regiment

Instructions regarding War Diaries and Intelligence Summaries are contained in F. S. Regs., Part II. and the Staff Manual respectively. Title pages will be prepared in manuscript.

Place	Date	Hour	Summary of Events and Information	Remarks and references to Appendices
BARCENAL (BELGIUM)	DEC 9th & 10th		The Battalion remained in billeting area BARCENAL – FAIYS. Bn Hdqrs at the CHATEAU de BARCENAL.	Ref Map MASIFE Sc. 1/100,000 RPA
	10th		The Battalion moved to area MOHIVILLE – SCY – SCOVILLE. Bn Hdqrs at MOHIVILLE.	RPA
	11th		Moved to area BONSIN – CHARDENEUX. Bn Hdqrs at BONSIN.	RPA
	12th		Moved to FILOT.	RPA
	13th		Moved to area WERBOMONT – BOSSON – OVENY. Bn Hdqrs at WERBOMONT.	RPA
	14th		Moved to GRAND HALLEUX. Bn billeted in INSTITUT JOHANNINUM.	RPA
	15th		Remained in billets at GRAND HALLEUX.	RPA
	16th		Moved to RECHT (GERMANY); crossing the BELGO-GERMAN frontier at POTEAU at 1210 hrs.	Ref Map I.M. (GERMANY) 1/100,000 RPA
	17th		Moved to HEPPENBACH – HALENFELD – VALENDER. (Bn Hdqrs at HEPPENBACH) and remained in that area till the morning of the 22nd	RPA

Army Form C. 2118.

WAR DIARY or INTELLIGENCE SUMMARY. 2/4 Hampshire Regt.

Vol XVIII

Place	Date	Hour	Summary of Events and Information	Remarks and references to Appendices
(GERMANY)	DEC. 22nd		Moved to area HUNNIGEN - HONSFELD. Bn H.Qrs at HONSFELD.	Ref. M.Ib. I.M. (Germany) 1/100000
	23rd		Moved to HELLENTHAL.	Rpt
	24th		Moved to KALL.	Ref. M.Ib. I.L. (Germany) 1/100000 Rpt
	25th		The Battalion completed the march at 1200 hrs on CHRISTMAS DAY, moving to MECHERNICH.	Rpt
	26 to 31		The Battalion remained in Billeting area MECHERNICH. 5 Offrs 139 ORs Joined Bn as reinforcements 26th LIEUTS. L.J. BOWEN, R.H. JONES 2nd LIEUTS. C.A.A. YOUNG, E. ALLEN D.C.M., F.E. HOLMES D.C.M.	

T. Brook
Lieut-Col.
Commanding 2/4 Battalion The Hampshire Regt.

SECRET.

VOLUME No 19.

Original.

"WAR – DIARY."
of
2/4TH BATTALION, THE HAMPSHIRE REGIMENT.

FROM:- JANUARY 1ST 1919. TO:- JANUARY 31ST 1919.

LIEUT. COLONEL,
COMMANDING 2/4TH BATTN, THE HAMPSHIRE REGIMENT.

FEBRUARY 1ST 1919.

Secret

Army Form C. 2118.

Original

WAR DIARY
or
INTELLIGENCE SUMMARY.

(Erase heading not required.)

Instructions regarding War Diaries and Intelligence Summaries are contained in F.S. Regs., Part II. and the Staff Manual respectively. Title pages will be prepared in manuscript.

Place	Date	Hour	Summary of Events and Information	Remarks and references to Appendices
MECHERNICH (GERMANY)	JAN 1919		The Battalion remained in billets at MECHERNICH throughout the month carrying out training of various kinds. A system of Recreational training was carried out into platoon batches. Christmas was celebrated in the Battalion (following training to be present) owing to the march to a place (moving) on Jan 29 Decorations were conferred on Lieut. F. Willis & Lieut. S. Limits + 2/Lt C. A. ROSSBAUM D.S.C. & C. BOWEN. 2/Lt E. ALLEN. Officers who re-embarked to the number of 34 during the month Officers rejoined from leave & re-embarkment R.D.	

J. Thompson Lieut Col
Commanding 4th Bn Hamps Regt

SECRET.

VOLUME No 21.

adjt MG R.72 / SOUTHERN DIV.

T. 19
2 sheets

WAR — DIARY.
OF
2/4ᵀᴴ BATTALION, THE HAMPSHIRE REGIMENT.

PERIOD :-

FROM :- 1-2-1919.   TO :- 28-2-1919.

R.P. Fenn Capt.
for MAJOR.
COMMANDING 2/4ᵀᴴ BATTALION THE HAMPSHIRE REGIMENT.

WERMELSKIRCHEN. —
28ᵀᴴ FEBRUARY 1919. —

Army Form C. 2118.

Vol XXI

WAR DIARY
or
INTELLIGENCE SUMMARY.

(Erase heading not required.)

Instructions regarding War Diaries and Intelligence Summaries are contained in F. S. Regs., Part II. and the Staff Manual respectively. Title pages will be prepared in manuscript.

1st Hampshire Regiment

Place	Date	Hour	Summary of Events and Information	Remarks and references to Appendices
Mechernich	Feb 1 to 22		Bn remains in billets area at MECHERNICH.	Ref Maps 2 x Germany 1/100000
				RPP
	23		Bn moved by rail route to WERMELSKIRCHEN, relieving 2nd Bn. HAMPSHIRE REGT.	RPP
WERMEL-SKIRCHEN	24 to 28		Bn remains in billets area at WERMELSKIRCHEN	RPP

R.P. From Capt. for Major
Commanding 1/4 Hampshire Regt.

D.A.Y.S.
1919

www.ingramcontent.com/pod-product-compliance
Lightning Source LLC
Chambersburg PA
CBHW081448160426
43193CB00013B/2409